TURTLE OR TORTOISE?

By Rob Ryndak

Gareth Stevens
PUBLISHING

Please visit our website, www.garethstevens.com. For a free color catalog of all our high-quality books, call toll free 1-800-542-2595 or fax 1-877-542-2596.

Library of Congress Cataloging-in-Publication Data

Ryndak, Rob, author.
 Turtle or tortoise? / Rob Ryndak.
     pages cm. — (Animal look-alikes)
 Includes bibliographical references and index.
 ISBN 978-1-4824-2728-8 (pbk.)
 ISBN 978-1-4824-2729-5 (6 pack)
 ISBN 978-1-4824-2730-1 (library binding)
 1. Turtles—Juvenile literature. 2. Testudinidae—Juvenile literature. 3. Adaptation (Biology)—Juvenile literature. I. Title.
 QL666.C5R96 2016
 597.92—dc23
                                    2015010119

Published in 2016 by
Gareth Stevens Publishing
111 East 14th Street, Suite 349
New York, NY 10003

Designer: Sarah Liddell
Editor: Ryan Nagelhout

Photo credits: Cover, p. 1 (background) ZoranKrstic/Shutterstock.com; cover, p. 1 (turtle) IrinaK/Shutterstock.com; cover, p. 1 (tortoise) xpixel/Shutterstock.com; p. 5 Aumza2529/Shutterstock.com; pp. 7 (terrapin), 21 Jay Ondreicka/Shutterstock.com; p. 7 (tortoise) All-stock-photos/Shutterstock.com; p. 7 (tortoise) Brian Lasenby/Shutterstock.com; p. 9 (top) Wayne Lynch/All Canada Photos/Getty Images; p. 9 (bottom) Andrew Bee/Oxford Scientific/Getty Images; p. 11 Paul Vinten/Shutterstock.com; p. 13 Drew Home/Shutterstock.com; p. 15 (turtle) Polly Dawson/Shutterstock.com; p. 15 (tortoise) ANDRZEJ GRZEGORCZYK/Shutterstock.com; p. 17 (turtle) Isabelle Keuhn/Shutterstock.com; p. 17 (tortoise) Serge Vero/Shutterstock.com; p. 19 (turtle) mrHanson/Shutterstock.com; p. 19 (tortoise) Kietr/Shutterstock.com.

Printed in the United States of America

CPSIA compliance information: Batch #CS15GS: For further information contact Gareth Stevens, New York, New York at 1-800-542-2595.

CONTENTS

Boldface words appear in the glossary.

What's in the Shell?

There's a short animal with a big shell in your yard. Is it a turtle or a tortoise? Figuring out what your new shelled friend is can be hard unless you pay attention to a few special things about each animal.

Family Findings

Turtles, tortoises, and terrapins are all **reptiles** in the Chelonia animal group. They all have hard shells called carapaces. Sea turtles are part of the Cheloniidae family and freshwater turtles are from the Emydidae family. Tortoises are part of the Testudinidae family.

TERRAPIN

TORTOISE

TURTLE

Same and Different

Many tortoises and turtles look very much alike. They both lay their eggs on land. You have to take a good look at their shell, legs, and where they live to tell the difference between the two reptiles.

TURTLE EGGS

TORTOISE EGGS

On Land

The biggest difference between turtles and tortoises is where they spend their time. Tortoises spend all their time on land. Some tortoises live in dry **climates**. Tortoise shells are rounder and help keep them safe.

Water Turtles

Turtles spend most of their life in water. Some live in the sea, while others live in rivers or lakes. Turtle shells are usually flatter, which helps them swim. Turtles can come on land for food, but many eat sea plants and animals.

TURTLE

13

Feet or Fins

Many sea turtles have feet that look like **flippers**. Some turtles that live in rivers or lakes have webbed feet. They use these flippers or webbed feet to swim quickly. Tortoise feet are short and round. They're only used for walking.

SEA TURTLE

TORTOISE

15

Nesting

Turtles and tortoises both lay eggs. Baby turtles and tortoises **hatch** using an egg tooth, which is a sharp point on their bill they use to break their eggshell. Sea turtles lay their eggs in sand. Their babies have to make their way down the beach and into the sea.

TURTLE

TORTOISE

HOW CAN YOU TELL?

ANIMAL	TURTLE	TORTOISE
FAMILY	Cheloniidae (sea), Emydidae (lakes and river)	Testudinidae
LAND OR WATER	mostly water	land
LOCATION	North America, Central America, South America, Africa, Asia, Australia, all oceans except the Arctic ocean	Every continent except Antarctica
FEET	flippers, webbed	round, short
LIFE-SPAN	up to 80 years	up to 150 years
SHELL SHAPE	flatter	rounder

17

Old Animals

Turtles and tortoises can live a very long time. Galápagos tortoises are some of the oldest living animals on Earth. Scientists have studied Galápagos tortoises that were more than 150 years old! Sea turtles can live up to 80 years.

SEA TURTLE

GALÁPAGOS TORTOISE

Terrapins

A terrapin is another member of the Testudinidae family that has a shell. What makes it different from turtles and tortoises is that terrapins only live on land and in **brackish** water. They live in **marshes** and along riverbanks near the ocean.

TERRAPIN

GLOSSARY

brackish: a mix of salt water and freshwater

climate: the average weather conditions of a place over a period of time

flipper: an animal's wide, flat body part that is used for swimming

hatch: to break open or come out of

marsh: an area of soft, wet land

reptile: an animal covered with scales or plates that breathes air, has a backbone, and lays eggs, such as a turtle, snake, lizard, or crocodile

FOR MORE INFORMATION

BOOKS

Gish, Melissa. *Tortoises*. Mankato, MN: Creative Education, 2013.

Shaskan, Trisha Speed. *What's the Difference Between a Turtle and a Tortoise?* Mankato, MN: Picture Window Books, 2011.

WEBSITES

Galápagos Tortoise
animals.nationalgeographic.com/animals/reptiles/galapagos-tortoise/
Find out more about the Galápagos tortoise on this National Geographic site.

Turtle & Tortoise
animals.sandiegozoo.org/animals/turtle-tortoise
Learn more about the turtles and tortoises at the San Diego Zoo here.

INDEX